SELECTED PORTRAITS

SELECTED
PORTRAITS

Poems by Ron Charach

WOLSAK
&WYNN

Cover art: John Brown, Grimm#40, 2004, oil on wood, 21" x 21", courtesy of the artist and Olga Korper Gallery, Toronto.
Cover design: Rachel Rosen
Author photo: Irvin Posluns

Typeset in Minion and printed by the Coach House Printing Company, Toronto, Ontario

The publishers gratefully acknowledge the support of the Canada Council for the Arts and the Ontario Arts Council for their financial assistance.

The Canada Council | Le Conseil des Arts
for the Arts | du Canada

ONTARIO ARTS COUNCIL
CONSEIL DES ARTS DE L'ONTARIO

Wolsak and Wynn Publishers Ltd
69 Hughson Street North, Ste. 102
Hamilton, ON
Canada L8R 1G5

Canadian   Patrimoine
Heritage   canadien

National Library of Canada Cataloguing in Publication Data

Charach, Ron
[Selections]
    Selected portraits / Ron Charach.

Poems.
ISBN 978-1-894987-20-2

    I. Title. II. Title: Selections.

PS8555.H39834A6 2007   C811'.54   C2007-905416-1

CONTENTS

THE BIG LIFE PAINTING (1987)

SOMEONE ELSE'S MEMOIRS (1994)

Past Wildflowers (1997)

Petrushkin! (1999, 2000)

Dungenessque (2001)

Elephant Street (2003)

THE INFLUENCE OF HANDS

Small uses of the hand strung out our lives
inside the family;
we should have spent days
loading piles of extra hands onto trucks . . .

Father fingered, nursing half a glass of Coke for hours;
Mother dazed over the laundry
listened hard to her arthritic reds
secretly shining her thin skin
peel me
tulip bulbs growing in the joint-space
wired to her complaints,
angry after every dish;
thanks for supper
said the painful crystals
as she peeled her yellow dishwashing gloves.

Brother would try his hand
cutting favorites out of the morning comics,
gluing them to cardboard to make figurines.
I kept my hands in view at the table
while underneath the covers
I jacked up my youth like a mechanic
and could plant dark silent bombs
for shocking returns . . .

Their laboring hands were more mindless
than unskilled:
Too quick to discipline,
they pointed at the stranger,
counted coins in the food
and packaged the remains of today's pasty meals
for days longer than a tongue could comprehend.

Only at the beach could we leave behind our hands:
Father – on his back, blowing out the spout of water
as a great pink whale,
Mother – lying body-long on the blanket,
even Brother – piling castles
and daring the undertow.

I stood thin and wavering
safe for a moment from hands
making signals behind my back, a final use of hands
to draw the coastguard into shore, with a plea:
Let us stay here forever, buoyed on a beach
where Dad can be a king,
Mom can loll like royalty
and we can all eat straight off the shells . . .

A POLICEMAN SMILES AT NOTHING

On one of those flannel nights
we awaken in fear, sensing
something is wrong with Mother,
whimpering just the other side
of the folding louvres.

By not doubting her sooner
we have forced her to cry.
Lucky Arthur always lapses back,
leaves me to watch the thin lit crack,
knowing that her moods are boiling dyes
in the other room.

Her plump arms are wired with nerves;
The Soaps move her, she rolls on coasters,
everything moves her but Father,
sleeping, deep in his helmet of a grade eight education.
I hear her humming to herself, a song she will not teach us,
Daddy, daddy, daddy, pin a rose on me!
By the time she collapses,
moonlight has percolated through the curtains;
I can finally visit the fridge.

Opening the great white door
to the bulb that beams
in the enamel body:
a bag of thawing white bread nests on chrome racks,
eggs relax in form-fitting chairs.
I think of worlds as clean as this,
where the freezer fills with heavy flesh
and the guard whirs, a policeman
who smiles at nothing.

Trying to wake up
like a bird in a pool of hot wax:
Father will work for more white bread.
Mother will rearrange the dust.
Artie will dress in remedial states of consciousness.
Even now Mother stares as she shakes her head,
My scratched waxed floors,
looking for signs –

THE MAN WHO FELL THROUGH

– How did you know that the ice was so thin?
– Well, my Daddy fell in,
  and he hardly weighed nothin' at all.

Surprising. That a man
who felt as hollow as a drained egg
could fall through. And at such an early age.
Say it: he lived a mean life,
his vocabulary geared to the using up of things:
he *burned* lights in the living room,
could recite three years of heating bills
month after costly winter month
like a parishioner rhyming off the saints.
After he died I put on a torn T-shirt
and walked around like his son.
Don't let the women steal your heart away,
They'll take whatever isn't nailed down;
clean you out like an enema.

What else could a kid of his have to lose?
He spent his nights stacking piles of pennies
on the arborite table, arranging, re-arranging,
the John-Paul Getty of the brown coin set.
Late at night, chief financier of a half-lit kitchen
he watched the clock use up his nights
the way the C.P. railway clocked his days.
In a night-duty uniform
of wife-beater shirt and underpants
nursing half a glass of Coke for hours,
red in the face,
a Vulcan to his little boys
unable to sleep in the adjoining room.

Now I stare at the fire
as it licks away the logs
and consider his warnings,
the dreary prospect of joining him.
May I never count blessings like coins.

My only car (his original body)

To start with a '72 green Dodge Dart,
to say, If my car had a head
I'd put a bullet through it:
Sorry, kid – but we can't guarantee this engine work;
Do you know that you had the original PCV valve,
THE ORIGINAL! You can't DO that!
I look at him like I've looked at hubcaps
I was just about to remove:
No *I'm* sorry;
this is My Only Car.

To make peace with Stradivarius brakes,
and temperamental door locks,
my car is a circus-at-the-wrong-time,
and It Wants Too
whenever they pay me more.
The only thing I added were beige covers
that slide off whenever someone fat sits.
One's father's car always runs better.

This car was my father's car for 45,000 miles
or his death.
Whichever came first?
I take care of it
the way he took care of his original body;
the car always follows the owner down.
This car has tried to kill me twice
since Reliable Motors tinkered with the brakes.

The license number is 278 IUB.
I remember it this way:
27 to 28; my age two years ago;
IUB – intra-uterine bebice,
this is a variety of word-play,
and I call the car Betsy
like my father did;
he treated objects like women.
He never had more than one car.

A NO-CONTEST FEELING (GOD OR SPADINA)

On Spadina, immigrants and vagrants
try to ignore each other
like intensive care patients
hooked up to a single monitor.
And the man in the huge gray army coat
who only fights internal wars
asks in the air for handouts.
The man who runs the discount art store
and insults all his customers, knowing
his prices are the best, says
"You knock over that easel,
you buy it."
On the slippery sidewalks
you watch for ghosts in the puddles,
residues of those who climbed straight up
from where their parents' weary horses gave way.
Rag peddlers became merchants
who made the city listen,
then moved East and North,
all the way to Retail.
Others have arrived to replace them,
slapping the air into currents
with their "sh" and "tch" languages
that stir up the fish smells
of their old-country homes.
And the gray local Royal Bank
tries to snare a few borrowers
from its line-up of labourers
come to cash their Friday cheques,
hypnotizes with a digi-screen:
Win a portable threat with every mortgage
you transfer to us ...

And the pizza-man with the black mustache
and the circus name, Massimo,
could serve pizzas worth killing for
but has to make them go around
to a hundred kids from the local school
so they lose their jet-black oven heat
and regress to the fast-food mean.
At the Clarke and the A.R.F.
and The Mission and The Silver Dollar
and even the El Mocambo, the God is Dead refrain
is played so many times
the Old World faithful clutch their crosses.

Follow a lone businessman
as he boards the packed Southbound bus,
standing among the white bargain bags
from Chinatown, bulging with noodles, bok choy
and the heady smell of fish,
to travel a distance of only three stops
just to steer clear of The Mission,
with its panning no-hopers.
Watch him enter The Bagel,
grin nervously at the too-familiar redhead
with the bustful of badges
who spreads so much cream cheese on
his pumpernickel
that his arteries stand on end.
Stepping onto the street,
grease staining through his paper bag,
he heads for the variety store, run by
'The only man in the world his size'
who *always* knows the price of Clorets,
and who can slip a girly magazine
into a long paper sleeve
in something just under a second.

Here a man finds immunity to pain,
can hang from the teats
or nest in the thighs of a teenage stripper,
like a festering rash.
Can merge with the pain
by holding closed his camel-hair coat
and looking straight out
over contrasting lives.
Like a man who has escaped his caste,
such a *no-contest feeling* comes over him
that he can step through the litter
on Toronto's last-remembering street,
as a king stepping over
his concubines

whose origins God or Spadina
only knows.

THE ONLY MAN IN THE WORLD HIS SIZE

You start off your morning
at the all-purpose store,
a confabulation of lottery tickets,
toiletries and adult magazines,
mainly to observe The Man.
A Yiddish Caruso at his register,
when you ask him how much the Clorets are
he chants the latest, like a cantor, *"Forty-Eight!"*
The only man in the world his size,
he goes to "The Bank" each day at 2 P.M.
and when he gets there, walks straight past the line
and heads for the glass booth at the back,
where *he tells them.*
He parks his wife at the lotteries desk,
won her after a kind of numbers game
of tatooed forearms
and odds of surviving
only a numbers man would go for.
His accidental escape,
had anyone noticed,
might have made fools of sadists.
He keeps registering fools,
fools who buy cigarettes instead of Havanas,
nervous souls who need a dirty picture
in the middle of a work day
(though The Man goes easy
with these types,
and says he *"understands … Some people …"*)
Once, when I tried rushing him
on a rainy day of streetcars worth chasing
he froze me in place with the words, *"You too."*
But all he needs is to make a few sales
and he pulls in his thickly bruised horns.

Once I heard him brag
that he and three other inmates kept their *Lager* so clean
that for two days the Nazis killed *Nobody.*
He only suffers to kill with a nasty look,
even takes the streetcar to work
though he could pick up an Audi or a Porsche
and still have change.
But by the end of the day
whatever his machine
it would turn into the same
Babylonian wheel.
Behind explosive laughs
and uncanny smiles
he hides his special powers: in dreams
he works a folksy version of this streetwise store,
one where Jews and Germans buy sausages together
without a second thought,
where the *Jude!* sign means welcome
in any language, and the hours he keeps
are humane.

Late at night
he floods his spotless house
with so many lights
that the Hydro keeps sending him
inappropriate Christmas cards.

But the only thing he cannot downplay
is his uncontrollable growth:
his wife already blended into his right arm
though moody, and too quick
to reach for a hanky;
and his son long ago became his right leg.

With his laboratory hours piling up like his Dad's
already he may have a kick
at the Nobel Prize.

He spends the early morning hours
after the wife is cottoned out,
binging on baked goods much to tempting to carry.

But the blender he uses
to reduce the separate chunks of life
to a custard of gain
by now has grown the kind of blade
that can make even sponge cake and heavy cream
bleed –

A POEM ABOUT THE PANCREAS

Even if you opened a practice on Harley Street
no patient would come in with complaints
about their pancreas:
"I think it's my pancreas, Doc!"
– unless they too are a fellow professional
also educated
out of their natural mind;
few patients are alarmed by the word,
not like the "heart,"
a word that summons the feeling 'the biscuit'
in the best of us.

Years from now
when you trundle in
thin and yellow, depressed,
for abdominal films,
you too will have forgotten
your pancreas; and the news "It's cancer
of the pancreas" will hit
like an old family secret you knew all along;
"I'm sorry, but it's cancer
of the sweetbread"
"Not the sweetbread!" – "Yes,
and, with proper medical management
early surgery
and a very rigid diet
you can look forward to at least
three months."
When the pancreas goes,
it goes.

Not even the diabetic
whom the pancreas
torments by degrees
can help us conceive
of that familiar; even a poet
is at a loss for metaphor;
nothing short of a surgical exploration
will unearth

the thick spongy worm
twisted twice on itself
buried deep in the viscera
silent behind its curtain of peritoneum,
with a head, a body
and a tail,
using the man's face.

THE MOST SERIOUS MOMENT OF OUR LIVES

Years later as Mindy began to unravel,
and rolled on the hospital floor
when she failed to get her way,
her second drink of lye
impressing not one soul
in her exhausted family,
they all agreed to
plug her into the wall
when the fourth and final round of pills
failed to work.
Wheel her back when you're finished,
head turned over on its side
so she can't breathe her vomit,
meaning no aspiration.

But when her eyes unsealed in the white tiled room,
and she hoarsely called for water,
she recognized my role in this,
my professional ring through the plastic.
She may have seen a liar straining
to escape from my face,
because instead of asking about her husband
and the kids,
and who knew,
and did everybody know,
instead, she turned her electric breath on me.
Automatically, I told her, "Shhh, It's okay now . . ."
but she looked me up and down and said, "This
is the most serious moment
of *our* lives."

SO YELLOW AND SO SMART

What *does* protect my heart from your *absinthe* breasts,
or the delicate tufts in your wet floral one-piece;
that my eyes do a half-lid when you say
that you come from The South?

If you think I stare, then ya shoulda seen Dad.

Dad would follow a girl up the slatted spiral stairs
weaving into boutiques
trying to find words. To this day I cherish his absence,
I worry that I look like him
when my tongue drips hollow lines
or my eyes start to wink on their own,

tracking,
– tomorrow you'll go sailing-instead,
and I'll trace you from a rock
that I'll have cut my feet to ribbons to reach;

riveting,
half the blood in my eyes by the time you're out,
squinting for a view past the buoys, you laughing off
the occasional spray, me,

praying for a wind to force you in,
for a ray so yellow and so smart
that you'll lean back

and remember this beach,
his sadder son watching from a generous three miles
in a court robe of skin, *Look at me – thin, and ribbed like a cage,*
and trying you.

Gravedigging at Lourdes

A glimpse of the Virgin is a glimpse of the Virgin.
To deny the dead man his white light,
to give up prematurely on the bored or decomposed –

If we could yank Dad above sea-level for a while,
prop him like a bolt
and then let the Holiest of Holies proceed to do their thing,
it might be the first time ever
that Dad could be said to be "Upright,"

if not truly cleansed,
if not forgiven
for his mock beatings, his exaggerations of what *was there*
(but exaggeration none the less) –
If we could transform that pile of payments
and suspect-prayers he was,
into that rare bird:
The Kind of Dad We Always Wanted –
But this is an age of final verdicts.
Lourdes has bottomed out
like France herself,
and an overdose of ragged arms reaching from graves
in grade-B movies
has left us numb;
and the never-fully-motivated Dad,
sinking back into our mental quicklime one last time
almost thanks us
for not redoing him.

I NEED A LARGE HOUSE

Inter urinas et faeces nascimur.
St Augustine

Pounding the stairs to the third floor on all fours
to settle an image fever . . . it takes a cathedral wall
to dam up silence, absorb the snores of innocence,
the whoops and bellows of cartoon characters, hoots
and hollers of game show contestants;
most of all, twin streams of sunlight and water
pouring through windows and shower heads
to stir the concentrate that settles
by very early morning.

My wife complains:
"This house is too big for a family of four,"
too big to heat, to clean – to populate.
She never knew me as "the rabbit"
in a house so confining that rage would ricochet
off the bare skin

into rinsed jars, pickle-jars, mustard jars,
jars that once held Mayonnaise: The proverbial *jars*,
like father, sturdy but tippable, hidden
behind open doors by day
serving as family latrines by night,
to be emptied next morning.
In dad's vernacular:
Lulu had a baby /its name was Tiny Tim/
she put it in a pisspot /to see if it could swim . . . "
The real toilet was upstairs, darkly monitored
by our skeleton-tenant Bryna
who never seemed to use one.

Entering a bedroom, you opened the door slowly, not knowing
who you might interrupt – knock over!
Only sizzle versus nozzle sounds to guide you:
mother, father, brother,
engaged in cramped and hasty physiology.

When a door did swing open all the way
and squatter's rights were not in play, the inevitable *clunk!*
of door striking jar, different notes
for empty or full, graded penalties, depending
on the pisser's rank.
But when a door opened in a dream
and the noise came back empty and no golden stream
came seeping across the beaten hardwood floor,
relief soon turned to despair,
as small predictable spaces came into view
but absolutely refused
to unfold.

Uncle Jake and the Card Game on Earth

Not to detract from the ravishing bride
or the pale Bar Mitzvah boy with his fistful
of envelopes, but at every family affair
we take time out to honor Jake The Elder.
*Not that I'm good-looking like our young
Master of Ceremonies*, he winks,
helped to his feet to toast
the proud parents.

Being the Elder
rented by branches of the family
for a holdover bottle of V.S.O.P.
and, though no thinker, great posture
for the eighty-three years
in a family of widows and rare, shrunken men.
Two separate shocks, his white metallic hair
and the priceless gold pocket watch on a chain.
But Jake's thirteen God-given years parted down the middle
when Father took us down to the basement
to tell this:
"*My* father, your *Zaidy* Abraham,
they called him Abraham the Angel,
Alev Hasholem (May he rest in peace),
sent me out into a stormy winter night
wearing my hooded jacket,
to ask your Uncle Jake for the money back
 – from the 'business loan'.
I turn up soaked right through,
 – Uncle's triplex – an upstairs steaming with men,
seven of Jake's cronies playing poker
for high stakes.
I'm shivering, my knock is faint
on the oak door, like an intruder.

And there's Jake Himself in a haze of cigar smoke
sipping whiskey and looking past me,
– *white-haired even then!* –
holding his good hand close, a joker
among men feeling for kings.
What loan? he laughs, dropping
another of Father's sawbucks
into the pile.

And so, "Go Home,"
it meant more black-bread-and-soup
or thinned soup, "*Go home!*"
the years all re-warmed anyway
because Mother was dead three years by then,
and the wrong brother was blessed
with a poker face
in the Great Depression."

But why believe a bitter man like Dad,
when the family *needed* an Elder
to make up for its lack of a history?
Besides, Father counted everything like coins,
might have envied Jake's ace hand
of forty more years of robust life
still to come, card games no one invited Dad to,
even as a grown man.

Now that they're both gone,
is it Heaven for Dad, wrestling Jake down,
their jackets off, suspender buckles snapping,
locking legs and grabbing at each other's hernias,

Dad pulling at that white hair thick as sun-bleached turf,
trying to pry Jake from his marked cards,
toasted black bread falling all around them
thrown from the top of the tenement stairs
by *The Hooded Boy*
who would grow up all over *his* son,
compressing everything that mattered to the bottom line,
never taking chances –

"Jake the Snake" was more like it.
according to my father.

HELEN ON FIRE

By morning she slept in
or sipped lukewarm tea.
Only at nightfall would Helen widen her eyes
beneath her long orange weedy hair
and hold court with the neighborhood kids,
most of her own barely visible
as legs on rickety stairs
to the third floor,
a world of lifting linoleum
streaked black and the smell of gas
escaping.

Beneath us a languid day
of catching bees in bottles
then shaking them till they whirred
into a raging machine.
This evening it was Helen on fire.
What you got from her
depended on moods
that shot out like flames.

We stood close
as she snipped a lock of dull hair
from a runny-nosed daughter,
asking us who had matches to lend her.
Little Royden, grand inquisitor of bees,
who snared them from hollyhocks
in poorly rinsed pickle jars only Dante could do justice to,
 – *he* had matches to lend her.

As Helen lit the oily wick
the stink of singed hair
curled up and backed us down the stairs;
I could hear my parents' warnings
about 'Welfare Helen' and her loose ways,
her endless parade of drunks,
as the cobra smoke assailed us
thick and sticky as poverty,
unavoidable as sex.

A smoking bird of ill omen
pursued me
as I tore down those stairs
for the dim yellow outside light
of my parents' home
where rotting wood got papered over
with a serenity of unmoving flowers
and where nights spent smoldering
were a private affair.

MR. ADAMOV
Call me Misha …

Saying "Hi, Sir!" to Mr. Adamov,
mammoth master of the hallway, and teacher of humanities,
lavishing ideas on anyone blind to his despair.
What slender man could have carried off
those enormous checkered three-piece suits,
the authentic silver watch on a chain?
Who else anchor a roomful
of posing kids straining to keep moving,
with Huckleberry and Gulliver
and the original cast of history?

Having never had the nerve to ask:

An only child of Russian Jews
(he *had* to be their only child)
with one parent as fat, as brilliant, though bitter,
heredity's laws insist bitter …
Named Misha by an aunt high on poetry,
ambiguous before his first word, a future genius
who would never write a book of his own,
too lost in thought to turn his teachings into fame.
He only knew one form of personal gain.

They assigned him the 'major work' class,
a studious pack of *Wunderkinder*
who looked down their glasses at those who ran cross-country
or bashed muddy dummies at spring training.
Taking on this bookish crew and their single-strand identities,
he refused to give them grades!

But instead bathed them in the gentle waters of the pass/fail,
encouraging pet projects and long walks by the river
so that heart-to-heart talks might crystallize
into missions.

But after school, his sea of words run dry,
who was there to come home to?
A family? A wife? A dog?
A cleaning lady who kept him ahead of his sweat?
His politics were left-wing.
Or two elderly parents who refused
to look each other in the eyes.
Wary of the shower, they lined up their pills like victims
and prayed that what happened to them in the death camps
should never hang over *Our Misha.*
He, watching snowy TV channels over *schnapps,*
She pasting green stamps in the cold summer kitchen,
each lying in wait for the other, poised
to shoot down any bright-eyed idea
with *What do you need it for?*

When the weekend arrived Mr. Adamov lay in bed,
the small of his back pressed to the mattress,
night sweat trapped in the reddened baby folds,
his mind abuzz with a neon of tunes
for the school's Maytime Melodies,
elegant experiments for the city-wide science fair.

He would sooner study someone else's memoirs.

Rolling over on his side, eyes lightly closed,
broad white back to the window, he hummed
a few arias from Verdi,
and allowed the human procession
to pass him through.

SEA LOTION

Ah, that imported European bracer,
Pineaud's Lilac Végétal
aftershaves from Paris like colognes . . .

Out front the solid stone façade
of the famous McIntyre Block
Uncle Syd planted his revolving red-and-white pole
to proclaim the opening of snipping scissors
and the spring of sleek black combs.
Where *schmatah business* presidents
could get the fringes trimmed on the busy streets
of their shiny heads, their cigar-stuck faces
fawned over by Latino apprentices
heating towels, cheerfully
honing straight-razors

to litanies, batted back and forth
between heavy thrones pumped higher and lower
– "adjusted" – in floor-to-ceiling mirrors:
sports scores: NFL, AFL, CFL,
AFL-CIO vs. Management,
tales of comeuppance,
of men suffering body waste
in strange and public ways:
"Piss on him, that bastard!"
"Kahk eem oon!"

"I don't care *how* many camps he survived!"
"Now he *kahks oyf de velt,* that sonofabitch!
Half the models on the street,
real knock-outs, with *tzatzkehs* out to *here!*
they drop by to see him, one at a time,
after closing – for *promotions!"*

Restless ringed fingers tapped out
the seething beat of the present against the past
on plush red leather arm-rests
a familiarity of rolled-up sleeves
under smoothly revolving ceiling fans.

As Moses Goldman, "Maishe", growled obscenities
at those who polish the golden Mercedes,
"Syd, believe me, I would never buy
a Krautmobile if it was the *last car . . .* "
"And they have the *nerve* to pull up in them
to *Schul!*
And to let their teenage kids,
– little *pishers* that don't even shave –
race those overpowered death-machines
up and down the Perimeter
as if life was cheap as *borscht –* "

"But Lemme tell you, there's no place
on this goddam Earth, if you'll pardon me, Syd,
where they drive as bad as Boston!"
"Montreal!" from a chorus of travelling salesman
sharing a life-chair.
"Shah, Shtiel!! – Boston! And Bostonnn it will always be.
Not only do they tail-gate halfway up your ass
with their *brights* on, but they expect YOU to *pull over
so THEY can speed by! Meshuggah!"*

But someone's beard croaks, *"Manhattan!"*
and what can anyone say . . .
Electric razors switch on to keep the peace
– four, six, eight at a time in the prosperous Sixties,
once-sacred hair cascading into silvery tufts
swept by a colored boy into
gleanings, of men forever wealthy,
the almighty insured.

Linen hankies came out all across town
the day they saw the CLOSED sign,
a note taped on the translucent glass:
that Syd had an explosion in his barrel chest
even he couldn't roll with;
cast adrift on that expansive sea
of manicky *entrepreneurs*
whose arteries twist the tap.

Played you, he did,
firmly massaging the tightly strung cords
at the base of the neck,
just after your whisking, prelude to the talc,
discreetly offering Irish Sweepstakes tickets
and the classical condom, then still illegal . . .
Most of all, with his tonic man smell
as he leaned his gut against you
to trim those last survivor-hairs up top
he knew to let you keep, antennae,
mementos . . .

And those imported European graces,
quinine hair tonic in the bright red bottle,
and bracer in the companion long-necked green,
after-shaves from Paris
like colognes . . .
even as they burned your face off
made you breathe so deep you almost forgave
those Frenchmen
who were too in love with life
to mess with Nazis –

Appointments at the Store

Once, Mr. Forzley,
buoyed on an after-church drink
told the keeper of his corner store, "Josh,
you oughta be president of the United Nations."

Uncle Josh,
you carried thick red sides of beef
twice your size; and Aunt Leah too,
though you looked like something she had budded
in her sleep.
Standing against a sea of rushing customers
you slowed them down with a good *schmooze*
and during the insane lunch hour
you were unflappable as granite
weathered by slums and an adolescence
stacking soup cans while the radio played
Standin' on the corner/ watchin' all the girls go by ...
Proud of never needing glasses, you kept a constant eye
on the mirrors; you could spot a bum, and spare him;
escort him out *before* he stole.
And you could check The Queen of England's milk.

But your wife's moods could skywrite,
even after the clouds had passed
and her week of dark silence finally ended.
Then she would inflate with ambition,
water, puffy eyes and cheeks,
bursting with laughter as she gave away
"*our* groceries".
And even though you would work when sick with the flu
you had to close down the store for her
and pressure the doctor
to do *something,*
mechanical,
electrical,

– because who could keep up with her
at ninety miles an hour
or drink from overflowing coffee cups
that tasted of *Joy* ,
her hastily rouged face
bloated so full
that all she needed was an hour of sleep
and she'd keep the kids up the whole night
on songs.
Mr. Forzley said, "Josh,
with a wife like Leah
they oughta award you the Nobel Prize."
And when your phone rang long distance, for her,
always her, he'd console you,
"Next time, who knows,
maybe Stockholm trying to reach you? …"

Sneaking from a torn carton of cigarettes
you once caught yourself
in the fish-eyed overhead mirror,
looking a third the size
of her beehive hairdo
and wondering
if maybe you had all this
coming.

My third best friend

My third best friend would get taken in
by any father who showed promise.
He let older men examine his money
while his own elderly father puttered
in the basement by an open furnace, forging
snake rings with ruby eyes, cursing in Ukrainian
at the Germans in both wars.
My friend sat through his mother's soliloquies
over dinner, suffering her with a listless passivity,
a paleness beyond hurt.
I spent evenings with him
in a parked car, holding a pale flashlight over a road map
trying to get him to open up.

One sunny morning I invited
my overcast friend in for coffee.
But when he pulled up his shirt
to reveal row after row of old parents' teeth
still gnawing at his doughy abdomen,
I waved *Stop!* and scrawled
the name of my therapist before passing out;
(a best friend's blood is
especially red.)

SOMEONE SLIPS IN A FILTER

Walking the levee with Armand, heading down
a friendship that convention said
was too physical,
when suddenly he heaves a flat rock at *el toro desolato*
and we watch the huge thing rise,
leaving its cocoon of boredom
with a mass summoning of thighs.
Armand skulks a few yards ahead
and the brush is so thick on either side
all I can do is feel.
He pursues the unlikely ideal,
mouths a blind mole,
and Armand flips it over with his boot.

"I may never make it
as a writer," says Armand,
"I have too much contempt to describe things."
Someone slips in a filter,
and the farms grow hazy;
conversations we might have had
yield to roaring groans
from the African game farm miles away:
two lions mating.

It is easy to head back
to the warm cabin wood
and the crackling fire,
leaving Armand to split logs in the sunset
in his mackinaw, dark brown hair and a love affair
with a woman who easily lifts canoes.
Tomorrow a twin-prop flies me back to the city.
But tomorrow is many miles away
and the end of the levee is receding
like the climax of an old dream,
and may yet drag us both beneath the horizon
like an avenging mole.

For days when we all are thin

On these bloated evenings
that fold over on themselves,
I will not take in a single new idea
unless it is accompanied by pistachios
(and Persian ones, at that,
which the Revolutionary Guard
may have tampered with,)
unleavened times, when even the sinewy arms
trumped up on high school monkey-bars
feel tethered to a fat future,
when enough *will* be plenty,
and I can hand down the old causes
like tight vests to younger men,
bless their slender hearts and heads.
Lazy-boy feet on the Ottoman
a 7-layer Dagwood on seeded rye
by my thickening side,
I lean for the TV and try to follow who's on first.
Till the sheer load of how much I've managed to eat
starts to hit,
punching out fatty tears
from deep within swollen lids.
Oh for those black-or-white days of 20/20,
days and nights of perfect symmetry
when all wars might yet be ended,
no matter how far away,
no matter how infinite the lines
of ravaging men with black mustaches.
For a time when we all are thin,
like ideals,
thin as the soldier's final gallon of blood
straining to keep his options open,

thinking if not thoughtful times
when the body would serve up its finest juices
to the brain,
as though that crowning place
were the godhead.

To see my friends

On late autumn nights I risk my car
to see my friends, to unwind
the mountain roads in rain
that transforms the nightscape
to an unyielding glare.
Oncoming brights try to sucker me
to an elaborate doom.
Inside are many small green dials
to reassure me, a technology to spurn
the low aching wish for completion.
Soon we will complete ourselves,
chart the blood flow of our very thoughts,
like these thoughts of my friends
that so reliably distract me;
I could be pulled in pieces
from the wreck.

Already they have arrived, well ahead of me,
ordering wine while they wait
and wonder what I'll bring along
from an independent life.
They have survived my whims,
have managed a consensus
from some critical percentage
of the adult world.
They fought alongside, if not with me
through the body wars
and the teenage fears, jerkily
navigating the thick North American cream.
I've watched them nearly drown,
 – still catch them stumbling through circus rings
brought to life again
'by the friendly folks at IBM'
See how they approach those who ignore them,

with their red bulb noses
and oversize shoes, barking,
'Are *these* our feats?'

We all watch the same programs,
have glimpsed far-off foreign lands
where other young men march arm in arm
with blow-up photos of their leader,
eager to secure the enemy's heads
for their leftist or rightist boots.
Yet somehow we survive
with less zealotry.
Does that make me bland and undistinguished,
a man no one would bother murdering,
with emotional shrapnel so mundane
it fails to excite the bloodlust
of an enemy?
Have I opened my nerves to the air,
'There is nothing left
worthy of reproach.'

And yet,
my friends sometimes throw me a long look
like foundlings who get photographed
but not fed, like refugees,
and call me enemy
 – for not joining or leaving the cause
or the club, for heeding or flouting
some universal curfew.

Yet each autumn,
when the red leaves start to compete with the yellow
for angles in the sun, far too late in my fear, perhaps,
but long before the bright white floods arrive
to reconcile me to the solitude
of my winter machine,
– I risk my car, to see my friends.

ONIONSKIN

My translucence makes words shimmer
the sheen of the uneasily erased.

Whose fragility makes me pray
as I surrender a creasable sheaf of poems
to the thick-waisted manager of The Print Stop
where copies are 15 cents apiece
and small orders get bumped
or passed like tissues to a groggy girl-Friday.
He challenges, "How did you run that *last* batch? They're *tilted*."
Does she wonder how, in an ever-expanding universe
she wound up jammed alongside this Original?

Though they both have skin, neither seems familiar
with flimsy pages filled with sparse lines.
Do they notice me trembling
at a crimson nail riffling my papers,
her licked forefinger deforming the page tops;
then a swift march as she sweeps the lot off the counter,
nearly tipping a styrofoam cup
stained with lipstick?

Would that they found me un-reproducible!
But Onionskin is mastered
as she presses each delicate face to the cool glass
and the bright green light flashes its judgments.
She checks her watch, gazing past the acoustic tile
for lunch on the horizon,
the rear pockets of her blue jeans bulging
as she shifts her shapely weight,
easing out some early-morning coffee gas
into the huge modern roomful
of machines.

She remembers me standing at the counter,
as thin red crescents spread along the margins of her ears.
Why regret what passes through us, faint efforts
that dissipate and can never be recalled,
except on skin?

A COSMOLOGY FOR CAPTIVE ELEPHANTS

Don't count him in
on any herd activities,
he's a solitaire, belongs inside
a cage of logs, chained to a diamond-shaped rock.
And when the slow cows saunter past
they don't even look at him,
sashaying in their wrinkled house-skins
their young reaching for their teats,
each with the support of five other females,
should he bash his way through
for a moment of freedom.
But what would such a moment
bring down on him?
Can he approach all six at once?
And what will the feeders and the handlers think:
This bull no longer fears or respects Man,
this bull has forgotten the sacred word, "Crush!"
Even the buckets of pellets we feed him
make him restless
when he should be
content.

What kind of life is this? I ask,
watching the night slowly pass,
my wife beside me, so deep in her pregnancy
that I am left worrying for two.
I want to wake her back to the world,
to tell her that the new cosmology is fear,
but she rolls over massively
with a drawling "Goodnight, Hon – ",
supportive, if entirely asleep.
so I ease back into my pen
of silence and valium,
my tusks going soft, losing air,
my trunk curled up
like a toy.

ON THE WORKING FARM

I take Samuel, our youngest, to the working farm
and stop us in front of the pigsty,
(a big mistake.)
This lanky *Oklahoma!* type
keeps whacking the rear
of a huge sow
trying to back her up
so the boar can make his move.
"That's the daddy pig," I explain,
but the Okie slides open the muddy gate
for the boar to muscle into position;
makes his sudden mount, our stormed eyes
widen to his swinging black bag,
his unsheathed poker
disappointing –

As we back away
into the hay-reeking barn,
there's another massive sow, she and her piglets
kept apart in separate stalls,
but within ear-splitting range of each other,

so the piglets squeal to heaven
as they smell her, and she heaves
against the rough planks
trying to silence
their chorus of hunger.
The second this tumult strikes
the reverberating key
of history,
Samuel looks up into my eyes.

WATERLINES

Holding my baby daughter
as she squirms and chortles
in the chest-high water of the sheltered bay,
her softness against me, nothing is
but the soft slap of waves
and a fade of others playing –

Soon we'll be blending with the Sunday evening blur
of red tail-lights snaking back to Metropolis;
we'll stop off after sunset at the burger assembly
waiting for the traffic to thin,
other families pulling up in campers,
their two-year-olds in trances, fathers so weary
they throw their car keys
in the trash-bin.

Back on the highway I watch her
in the mirror, my darling little charge
content in her custom seat
even as the deer-fly bites start swelling
under her soft cotton shirt.
Finally she surrenders,
and will miss the last hour of our journey.
This dark, it is my own more than hers.
Hers is more a perfect skin
flawed only by vaccination;
though there is none
against what lurks
in the long cold waters.

In the House of Steaks

Into
the fabled dining house of two square rooms
whose manager tried to go out of business
but was bought out by his own clientele,
forced to stay open for unparalleled steaks.
Where you are serviced by waiters, so attentive
they almost notice you are there,
plunking down plastic bowls, a flask of oil,
a flask of vinegar – "You mix." – with cunning food familiars . . .
Here they serve up the prime steak naked,
filet or New York strip,
meat it is not legal to buy at the supermarket,
meat the poor will never encounter
even in their choicest dreams . . .
They serve it without fanfare
or so much as a sprig of parsley,
in this carnivorous paradise
graced by the rich and the bitchy
who find the portions skimpy in nouvelle cuisine,
who like to eat Chinese,
but have a primal need
for steak and potatoes . . .

But I have the worst seat in the house
facing the swinging door to the kitchen,
a toothless old crone moving back and forth
with a scalding pot, in a paper kitchen-help hat.
My choice of views:
four sullen and identically Spanish-tempered
Chinese waiters, standing at the back
waiting for Visas,
red linen over their arms concealing weapons;
a smoky aquarium of long-tentacled lobsters
climbing over their rich brothers,

deliberate as tanks,
while a man with a silvery mane watches one
getting hauled out, and demands,
"Did you weigh that in or out of the water?"
and, in large letters, instructions
on what to do in case you choke.

From my wife's better view
loom sullen wrought-iron pastoral lanterns
suspended from a bare ceiling of acoustic tile,
hanging against walls as red as blood.
A circular bar with a TV – for those lining up
(there are no reservations) – gives the place
a suburban-Vegas feel.

I double-take on the menu prices, then gape
at the parade of furs in the coat-check room
that would make a robber forget the register;
till the Advent: a proud sixteen-ouncer
of charred meat beneath a mountain slide of onion rings
and Idahos sliced tightly
still in their skins . . .

You can almost hear arteries twist shut
as you polish off your plate. And later, prime burps
that make you reminisce on the meal . . .

For dessert we watch four or five beefy men
looking like Normal Mailer out with his mother,
scowling past the unmoving line;
assorted species of WASP, more likely would-be WASPs
savoring the steak smells like country-club air.

And though none can join the Granite Club,
and all have family sitting it out back home
in Russia, or suburbia, with changed last names
that won't close doors to university,
they seem not to notice us
or the sleeping baby we brought with (we mistook
The House for a family eatery).
A single glance from them would warn
just how deep into the shadows
of these meaty urban hills
we've dared to venture
this time.

REMEMBERING: THE FIRST ROUND
1977, in a non-teaching hospital

On Rounds with the Staff man,
(a nice enough guy in his own way)
at the bedside of a 26 year old man
with a mustache – clearly gay,
and looking up in exhaustion and fear
because we are about to discharge him.

He has night sweats, really bad ones,
is losing weight
and has a golf ball in each groin.
But the fancy tests we run
all come out negative;
he's been in hospital a week,
and his biopsies haven't told us much.
"I can't go home like this;
I'm dying! he rasps.
But the senior Staff man shakes his head, (We're sorry.)
and on our way out deadpans,
"This guy's a *faygel.*"

Remembering his pale, sweaty face,
those painful groins, and the terror in his eyes –
the Staff man's unswerving calm, even levity
as the Specter of AIDS – *who could imagine*
the span of its mantle –
passed over us,
having made a first-round
Selection.

Note. *faygel* is Yiddish for 'a birdie'.

Colonoscopy

What could be cleaner or merrier
than to clear a dusting of snow on a crisp sunny day?
But this morning I visit The Rudd for routine colonoscopy.
Two days ago at the pharmacy I joked about my purchase:
two clear bottles of Citromag and three tins of eggnog Ensure:
"I'm going to a really wild party!"
"Yeah, Right!" laughed the pharmacist.
It won't be a picnic.

There is something cleansing
about volunteering. Something reassuring about knowing
exactly how much waste *this* body can contain.
And the brochure, praising courage, promises
that the laxative preparation is the worst part.

Unseemly, to talk about fires raging out of control
on an area no bigger than a quarter,
to draw more attention there than you have to,
but by the morning of the test I wonder
if I'll ever sit again –

Today I am to know myself
better; insights ten years of psychotherapy
haven't provided,
to plumb the inner furrows and folds
in search of some Jabberwocky polyp
to ensnare and burn away –

The clinic is a field of a room sectioned off
with plush furniture in themes of brown and beige
on a carpet the color of toast.
A nurse in crisp white uniform
hands out the inevitable forms.

I write down practically nothing:
as a teen some "irritable bowel" (whatever that means),
but add: Mother died of cancer of the coecum.

Dispassionate faces in the waiting room;
some have been through this many times.
At forty I'm here early, more imagining than ill,
but across me sits a black-haired youth with a colitis look,
his face gray as ash, his mother wearing her worry.

Yet I am chosen first,
and am soon up on a tilting table,
having decided to "pass" on the sedation,
(At three o'clock, I have patients of my own to see.)
"That's my finger," says the good G.I.
calling to mind more than one off-color joke,
and in an instant, he launches
five *yards* of limber, greased technology
as I try to relax and be a good sport.

(two weeks earlier,
a friend of mine went
to have a hemorrhoid lanced:
smiling Oriental specialist,
in Hirohito glasses;
anaesthetic injected: *ouch!*
infused, but *OUCH!* at the scalpel swipe,
the prostrate one tightening up,
fighting back with his last bit
of available muscle,
as above his shoulder, the doctor starts to shriek:
"You oppose me! You oppose me!!")

Forget such stories, in the name of deep breathing,
hatha yoga
– relaxation therapy;
as a million dank villous fingers clamp down
to slow its progress,
and are promptly overruled.

But negotiating the great splenic bend is more than I bargained for,
I grow shocky: *If it's all gonna be like this, then I quit!*
adding: *"Is it too late for sedation?"*

But the nurse pats my sweaty back,
as the sleek craft noses deeper into inner space.
Suddenly I feel for *"The Pain is Real"* victims,
for the gaunt young man in the waiting room
flipping through *New Yorker* cartoons for answers;
for abandoned old duffers
curled up on their cots,
everywhere.

But relief comes quick to the healthy;
turning over for the transverse portion of our journey
things start to ease up, even as air shoots in
so the man can do what he's paid to –

We're finally in the coecum; for he asks the nurse
to "wiggle the coecum", (*my* coecum) – another first experience.
This is the place that killed my mother.
I hold my breath. What if he lingers . . .
"Hmmm," he says, "Let's give this lens a wash."
But soon we're on our way out to brighter land,
where we need no fiber-optic light
and corners are turned easily.
A wad of tissue is left in place,
for the mopping up.

"I'm sorry if I gave you a rough time," I say,
getting dressed in my propriety.
"Oh, I think it was *us* who gave *you* the rough time," he replies,
then announces,
"You're clean."

FAILURE TO THRIVE

If only there were but one way to fail,
a hapless baby or two
lacking the know-how
to suck, breathe and swallow
at the same time.

Instead, is this progeny of souls
who received no love,
so can give none,
legions of near-retarded moms on welfare,
a drunken father on a park bench
and an ex-con boyfriend
who likes his women fat
and afraid.

They cannot heat bottles
they clutch at cigarette logjams
and drown in a sea of beer
the truck discharges at their door.
And if they water down baby's formula
it's because "everybody has to make do,"
baby's developing brain too.

Elvis, belt that corny line,
"He'll grow to be an angry young man
some day …"
He'll break his mammy's heart
his sweetheart's jaw
and some kind of record
for putting fists through walls.

For now,
we notify the Authorities
when the solitary mom fails
to show for the follow-up.

Oh, you sunken-eyed kid
with the big round head
and the "preemie look"
pulled so early
from the promised land of infancy,
one wintry night
I saw your nurse come alive,
no, *thrive*

when you finally kept down
all your feed,
and your great big eyes
started shining.

WHITE LACES
I'm not going to start a fight
unless someone else does.

He's only fifteen, but looks weathered
in an inked-on blue jean jacket,
his blueberry Doc Martens spanking new,
self-executed haircut, but nonetheless good-looking
in a James Dean way, with an intelligence
that's average, a potential under average,
and a hard time getting keen.

Admits he's a target
for the cops –"The Beast" –
and any rival gang that happens to be out.
"White laces means White supremacy."
(Were these calf-high risers once a polio shoe?)

Says it's worse in the wintertime
when the snow turns to gray slush
and everyone's freezing their balls off
and feeling down, and looking for someone
to take it out on.

How can he just walk away from the street
when all his friends
(each more fatherless than the next)
run with gangs?
Skinheads in Mohawks,
Mods with the checkered sash,
B-boys in oversize hats and dark skins
combing the city streets,
not one with a plan
for tackling this week's
homework.

Easy for me to say settle down.
He knows all the Metros by their first names.
He was there at The Ex on Black Sunday
when they bowled over everyone
and ran off with a thousand bucks of stuffed animals.

He downplays his knack
for finding instant brothers.
"I can't just go out and buy new friends
at the Eaton Center, now can I, Doc?"

I look down at those laces
festooned over steel-toed boots
and, unable to think construction,
feel his point.

SHE WILL NO LONGER TAKE HER FOOD

She will no longer take her food.
That she, the perfect eater in the family
would suddenly turn this bad . . .
Tomorrow, the doctor threatened,
they'll feed her through a tube,
or she'll just have to take her food by vein.

Today is September 4; as I see it,
they have another month
because in mid-December our family goes to Nassau
– been going for years –
if her weight doesn't climb by October
we whisk her straight to The Mayo.
That she should do this – she,
the dearest, most accommodating little thing
on Earth.
She must know she's hurting us!

But the tube, though greased
would go down no further.
They reeled it out,
said they'd try again later
and her blue eyes glared;
as they left,
her mouth once rigid as a vise
formed a perfect 'O';
a siren pulling at her hair, and then,
the overdetermined scream.

LABOUR AND DELIVERY
When lions are too close

My wife and I enter
the labour-and-delivery room,
a young wildebeest in her loins
to be birthed before the lions come.

But the hospital is our savannah,
and the nurse drones on
about working through her coffee break
and lays out on the green drape:
two vials of synthetic hormone
two sets of surgical gloves
an amniotomy hook,
then sixteen
surgical clamps,
one for every feeling we arrive with,
to turn the natural into the man-made,
the man-brought-on.

Is this one more dig at organized medicine?
Or have we tried too soon,
only to discover that backing up that happens
when lions come too close?

Ours and Yours

When we've created a sister for our toddler son,
accomplishing that miracle *one of each*
in a family known for a paucity of girls;
when the labor's gone smoothly
as such monumental straining goes,
all taken in by dad at his brave wife's side,

then the fact that next curtain over
in the semi-private suite
the couple who speak only Ukrainian well
had a baby with "a prolapse of the cord"
now doing badly in Intensive Care
– is just a fact.

No cause to cut into our joy
except for momentary twinges
when we pass their closed curtain
on visits.

And then that thank-God reflex:
once again the wheel of doom
has not landed on us
or ours.

DADDY-DAUGHTER LANGUAGE

My eight-year-old ambles into our bedroom
and announces she had a dream
she was running a little restaurant
called *The Particular Husband.*

Only yesterday out of an old white stocking
she made a baby duckling
that very nearly came to life,
and out of pipe cleaners a miniature girl
who did, then drew a floppy-legged
character in a huge hat, she called Mr. Blissful.

Dearest fellow namer of things
who, like your Dad, speaks in tongues,
what we call daddy-daughter language,
hold on tight to your mother's
and brother's practicality,
don't be tempted,
don't turn your life
into a performance piece.

At catwalk level

Up into the stratosphere we scramble to arrive
before the anthems, wondering if the peanuts guy
or the drinks guy ventures quite this high.
Three rows ahead a group of teens in face-paint flash and gurn
and pretend-fart in each others' faces to gross out the girls,
no sense of home to shatter
up here at catwalk level.

I loll through the game, my daughter content
with two ice-cream flavours curled upwards
in suspended flame,
and would rather we were at a world poetry competition,
the Irish versus the Jews,

perhaps back in the office consoling the songwriter
so painfully aware of his young heart beating
he no longer relishes being alive.

As the rain begins to fall we gather our kids, and leave
during the home team's at-bats, wishing the score mattered.

There is nothing I know better than these two little hands
I lead down the wide emptying ramps of heads.
Then the sleepwalk to a train, a parked car, a home;
all the vestiges of a life one would miss
not having lived to the end,
even in the worst times, even from the perspective
of too high a seat.

Psychiatrists on the subway

One rarely spots psychiatrists on the subway
rubbing the haze of a long day's sessions
from their lean temples,
or thumbing through paperbacks that deal
with anything-but.
Wouldn't they like an update on who's
in the world and how they're doing?

Or would the ridership be wary of men and women
whose briefcases rattle with the *tic tac*
of pills, whose ears perk
like armadillos' at conversations
two seats over?
More likely we locate them in a bad joke,
in a wing-chair beside a firm couch,
a suicide statistic, a product seminar
with deli sandwiches courtesy of Pfizer or Roche
or Eli Lilly;
perhaps on the beach of a convention hotel
with a panorama of thong-clad beauties
who seldom talk revealingly.

Before bed a psychiatrist sets his ears
on the night-table
and prays for a night of long silence
from a god who prefers
to listen.

Naming the Blue

What could be brighter than the blue
of this ice-cream truck, idle
as a day of steady rain?
But what kind of blue is it?
Neither peppermint, nor cerulean,
no, more like what *Pepto-Bismol* is to pink.

But what if it turns out a prosy 'cyan'
or worse, a false colour
without a proper name, a PMS-162?
For now, it matches the cap on this new bottle of conditioner,
I'll run it by Steve, who's in graphic design.

It's an answer you need,
a small gift
after a dull day when only one colour pushed through
with the urgency of
"forever" or "brilliant."

That's it, "brilliant blue",
colour of the sleeping pill zopiclone.
Like its cyborg name, it leaves behind
a metallic taste, but deep-blues
even the most barbarously
colorful day.

MRI

Nothing left, no more futuristic tests
to light up a world of misfiring sensation
and surprising pain

In the MR waiting room, in gown, pants and booties,
a small-town long-hair returns from the test,
"It was nothin' – " he brags, " – like bein' *inside* a Pink Floyd CD."
But the elderly lady warned,
"Those MRI's are the worst."

Questioned for rings, watch,
recent operations, metal clips, pacemakers –
I'm rollered into a cool-white plastic chamber,
a huge laundromat dryer, wind tunnel
with only a few inches'
clearance for face, trunk and arms
– claustrophobia,
prematurial burial.
I await the draw of The Magnets,
their Holstian 50,000 times the strength of gravity
to line up *all* my hydrogen atoms,
bombard me with radio frequencies
and scan every change.
Magnetic Resonance Imaging
photos as perfect, as cadaverous
as those in the *Atlas of Anatomy.*

I wear earphones.
Already I've known the CT Scan,
its crazed drumbeats followed by
ten thousand pounds of hamburger grinding.

The technician warned:
"You'll hear knocking noises, then a drilling sound
that will last one to four minutes.
There will be knocks like premonitions,
then an electroshock *vibrato* will shake you to your core
and redefine 'heart-throb', 'incessant' and 'compelling'.

You'll breathe at ever-higher volumes
without *daring* to move, waiting for the
hovering craft to leave.
Think of your body as a tooth
encountering a five-story drill.
Think of this as your biggest-ever brush
with high tech."

After the longest minutes life offers,
I vow to refuse the next fifteen.
Yet when they wheel me out
and ask "How ya doing?"
I answer, "Nothin' beats it."

Note. This poem was written before the arrival of the 'open-concept' MRI.

VISITING THE WHALES
Oh those disappearing, reappearing tails . . .

Motoring into Massachussets Bay on the Portuguese Princess,
on a salt-spray day, we forget that we awoke
in separate beds.
Our hearts clamor for the drama
on the cover of the brochure, a whale *breeching*,
an almighty third of its body thrusting from the water.

But what if a leviathan rises *under* our boat?
You hush me: "They're not stupid.
Quite the opposite."
Though we learn, ten minutes out, that the last group
saw a whale with propeller marks on its back.
"Since we turn off our motors and coast
it couldn't have been one of *our* boats . . . "
It's humpbacks we're after, smaller than the great blues,
killers or baleens, but *active*,
shooting whooshy spray out a blowhole,
a "whalatosis", quips our round-faced guide.

A sighting! We are not alone!
Two rubber submarines in synchrony,
massive faces black-barnacled,
rotate in slow motion
to display sleek white flippers.
One rolls over to show
his broad and polished back,
then launches a tremendous snort
of living spume!
(Can this be? Are they trailing lines of food
to draw them closer –)

"Honey, you *missed* it!"

"Well, *someone's* got to take her to the bathroom!"
That's what comes of making eyes at the sunrise,
first glimmerings of long days
pouring juice, drying tears, treading water . . .
She gets fewer nightmares than I do,
can go down sooner, for longer,
so that we often sleep in tandem.
By day we settle for a tidiness,
a comfort of perfect yellow bedspreads
tucked around crisp
white sheets.
But oh, those flashing tails!

THE GARDEN OF MY WIFE

My wife wraps her long fingers with ferns
and tickles me with astilbe.
She cloaks the ground in periwinkle
and seamless green-white lamium.
The shade she feathers with dogwood,
ninebark, and spirea, greeting the morning
with day lilies in hot lemon, russet
and champagne.
Out front, columbines trumpet
the Japanese maple,
basking in light by wrought-iron
winding with Virginia creeper.
There is a more stately side.
Three mitred yews preside
over sculpted *sedum spectabile*
which softens the huge Muskoka rocks
that further widen
our cracked-stucco farmhouse
in the city.

What have I added?
A centurion row of hostas to slow the run-off,
a couple of globular yews
to hold court by the front door
alongside the burning bush?
Was I wrong to suppress her desire
for lush peonies and Annabelle hydrangea
even as I cheer her frail clematis
up wooden trellises
and wish her every rosebush well?
Her short-lived irises
more than once saved my life.

What a reluctant ornamental onion
in the garden I am, to say yes
to only two seedlings
when she always wanted three.

THANK YOU

Dear gnarly-fingered lady
with the yellow-gray hair
who scales the fifteen stairs
to our doctor's by sheer will,

in the waiting room you scan *Time* and *Life*
with a magnifying glass and light
while we secretly look on,
already feeling healthier.

ONE LAUGHING UNCLE

Long after uncle Saul died, auntie Shailah boasted,
"My Sarah's vorkin', my Hannah's vorkin', my Allan's vorkin' . . . "

Uncle Saul, by trade an electrician,
in his late-thirties grew afraid of heights,
and holed himself in his room
with all the English classics
and dozens in Yiddish, Hebrew and Russian,
many of them humorous,
while his plump, pretty wife
trudged through snow in leaky rubber boots
door-to-door, business-to-business,
drumming up subscribers for
The Western Jewish News
to feed their three children.

Uncle, what makes an electrician fear
his heights, turns muscles into achy dough,
keeps him from driving a car,
owning a home, stripping paint
from a door?

Limping through my own late forties,
wife and children eating well
but without a taste for herring, black bread
or prune juice in scalding water,
I look away from
his body's insurrection,
the explosive laughing at his own jokes
and beet-root shape,
his borscht-belt surrender.

OUR LADY OF THE BUMBLEBEES

You are sunbathing on a worn red blanket
in the tiny yard backing the Burrows house.
It's Sunday morning,
and Dad, as usual,
is off at his older sister's
eating Sabbath leftovers.

Your lovely tanned face – my face – is turned to the sun,
long lashes closed, nostrils slightly flaring
as you revel in a prairie summer day.
Around you flurry bumblebees,
alighting on the dandelions and clover,
buzzing near your slender feet,
flying low over the bare arms glistening at your sides.

Rows of sticked tomato plants and luxuriant rhubarb
take up a third of the yard to the edge of your blanket.
Some mornings I watch you putter in the planted shade,
turning the soil, pretty as a sweater-girl with a watering can,
ignoring the bees and long-legged wasps
– while older Artie and I run like the dickens
whenever one comes at us, screaming *"Beenen! Beenen!"*
a made-up Yiddish word.

Now and then, across the wide-spaced fencing
the Ukrainian *babushka* next door dispenses gardening advice,
"Dis is veeds; *dat* is no veeds."
In exchange, you use Ukrainian words you've worked
to pronouce, the usual weather banter:

"Tepleh! Zimneh!"
"It's hot out! It's cold!"
"Mozshe dozshe; mozshe schnee."
"Maybe rain, maybe snow,"

jewels in your cosmopolitan crown
that always make the neighbors smile.
Though after we were given carrots from their garden,
you bade me surpass you, sending me off
with a memorized mouthful,
"Moya mama khazala zshankuyu za morkvah."
"My mother would like to thank you for the carrots."
making up for decades of Old Country anti-Semitism
that was, in the end, who knows whose original sin.

Backyard beauty of many tongues, are you the one
I would later call Lady of the Dumb 'I Love You's,
because you seldom came to my defense,
though you loved me,
you, who never made it into the history books,
but modeled for us
a solitary poise that was its own reward,
Our Lady of the Bumblebees.

A FRIEND FROM THE DEEP SOUTH

With graying blonde hair
and neatly trimmed goatee,
you're charming as Shelby Foote, narrator of *The Civil War*,
and though overactive with tics and twitches,
you're a Cotton-eye Joe on the dance floor
sweeping other men's wives off their feet.
Yet you tell me how, one night,
on a deserted beach in the Pacific
you and a lover were *wakened*
by the light of the Milky Way.

Next morning after a long swim
lazing on a slab of granite
overlooking the lodge,
you nod at a huge flat rock
that lilts with each incoming wave.
"Ah've never before seen a big rock
placed so it moves like that."

Same morning, you subtly indicate
a tall blonde in a burger line-up at The Sizzler.
She's wearing a see-through cotton dress.
"Do you think she knows it is?" I ask,
and without thinking, you answer,
"You bet."

PIONEERS OF PUBERTY

To Laurence Inch,
who after a long summer
debuted in nude swim with a thickened root
fringed by a shock of red filaments
from which tautly hung a pair of golf balls,
yet, for all that, wound up
one of the shorter males in our class,

To gawky Kathy,
whose nubile party-hats beneath a long neck
the boys found irresistibly funny,
and Belva, so maternally endowed
we couldn't pry our eyes away
from her areolar stare,

To my own neotonous group of three,
prepubertal to the bone, advocates of the silly,
who tried, with flashlights
under bathroom-lock
to speed the stubborn mystery,
boasting prematurely,
"Haven't *you* creamed yet?"

as though it were a subtle variation
on pissing, and not a shock
to the system to send us reeling
to a recovered older brother who would smile
and say, "yup – that sure sounds like it."

A moment of silence
for those who made their fellow children mothers,
for those forced to open their slender thighs
to surgical equipment and scorn,

for the misconceived
whether born and poorly mothered,
born and surrendered,
or forever and ever unborn.

MILLIONS OF *YAHRZEIT* CANDLES

All around the world
millions of *yahrzeit* candles burn
for my father, who never heeded
the high-flying breaths
of a red mackerel sky.
Smoke wafts from the mouths
of passers-by whose lips are parched
as if they would flicker my father's name
if it suddenly came to them.
Some have small-vessel disease yet smoke on
even through amputations.

Like them, Pa rolled "pills",
stringy tobacco in ultra-thin *Vogue* papers,
slim pillars in a barely balanced life,
and nursed a late-night glass of Coke as he prepared
for another night-shift in the windowless basement
of the high-domed railway station,
breathing in and out his own smoke
like the burning bush raging
against its confinement
that he was.

HAL

How many are there like you,
awkward six-four mantis frame,
your head towering above the crowds, or folded
high-kneed on a seat in an endless subway,
a last worn volume of Dostoevsky to your name?
You changed appearance with each mood,
a *series* of brilliant heads:
some hairy, some shaved,
each anguished, and somehow off the mark.

Your inventions!
A straw hooked up to a vacuum cleaner
pulled snot faster than a head-cold could replace it.
And your performance art:
a slide-show of wrinkled blank pages, magnifications
of things no one would dream of showing,
set to music.

Your suicide, long predicted, felt sudden,
like the white-water rafting
you tried once on a lark,
complete strangers howling across from you
as you offered your finely shaped skull
and proud tartar cheekbones
to cool passages
marked by rocks.

THE DIET OF STEFAN

A Vegan and a rawist, Stefan lives exclusively
on green peppers, tomatoes and nectarines,
has nothing but contempt for
"dead vitamins and minerals
the body cannot use."
Warned by his physician ex-wife in '85
that he would be dead within a year,
he approaches the millennium in triumph
laced with dread.

Once he confided that he had "psychic bangs".
"Pangs?" On being corrected,
I thought he meant those small but complex universes
spawned by the unconscious mind.
No, these were errant tendrils of brain
that festooned his eyes
whenever his bony skullcap
was pulled away with force.

He made me think of Luther
at the Diet of Worms,
judged by the Western world
yet recanting nothing,
warning his interrogators
how dangerous it would be to ignore his conscience.
Spirited into safe hiding
by Frederick the Wise,
he rewrote the New Testament version
still used by the Church that bears his name.
Later, as if struck again by internal lightning,
he preached Death-to-the-Jews
for their failure to ingest
the newer, more wholesome
homilies.

PETRUSHKIN!

We are spinning on a globe, Petrushkin,
where the ultimate Disney set
is Alcatraz Island,
where thirty-nine Heaven's Gate cultists
shed their Earthly containers seeking to hitch a ride
on a spaceship behind the Hale-Bopp comet
to a new home near Sirius.

A cloudy blue globe whose spin no one feels
but melancholics on a switch day
or burned-out manics recalling
the high-flying ways.

Even you, spectral Petrushkin,
thimble-sized in a pseudo-Russian hat,
white scarf unfurled like angel wings
twirling on the end of my flaky thumb,
swirl an unfamiliar potato smell
with orange and yellow halos around black balls
that lure nerve-doctors to my temporal lobes.
See how they parade in starched white coats
and keep me up all night
and crown my scalp with needles
in the hope of catching a trace of you
bald-faced, wide-eyed,
mid-parody –

PROSTATES GROWING

No man-hating avenger
could situate it better,
turgid bulb at the root
and no old man's friend;

reclining, bearing down
till the once proud
early morning fount
is strangled to a sizzle.

In silence after heavy rain
you can hear prostates growing,
or being staved with rinses
that turn the hair jet black,

irrigation lines that nourish transplanted hair
or trips to the squash court
squeezed around days
designed to be tubular.

Just as we go to the ball game
to see the players looking bigger
and smaller,
we hope to make it through

the operation under spinal block,
the last great reaming of the body
a man's mind can
comprehend.

THE REVIEW THAT KILLS

The review that kills finds the poet at home
alone on a wintry night, furnace on the blink,
three months into a trial separation,
his best friend – so he thought – departed,
two thirds into the second six-pack,
trying to recall better reviews from the past.

Who is this 'crickit' who pens the review that kills?
A fellow amateur failed in love or art?
A woman with impossible standards,
an ex-lover with a grudge?
Another expert trying to stake a claim?
Is it the man who, asked if his journal would consider light verse,
answered, "Not as long as I am editor."

After the burial, friends and acquaintances denounce
the review that killed; how a sensitive man
with whom they had shared the six-packs of respite
succumbed to a masterful blow
at his history and quirky humour,
the un-ethnic way he spelled his first name,
how he refused to write mainly for his own tribe
and be one more minor poet
from a mountainous village overseas.

Friends gather for a few drinks and a memorial reading,
of the very work that was savaged,
silently comparing their own poems
to those of the unsung martyr, dead
by his own tippy hand, by something
approaching choice;
while somewhere, in the lull
of one more passing season,
the same devout reviewer reloads –

SOAPSUDS

Young Samuel scoops
palms full of soapsuds
then wipes them off on me,
laughing his head off
at my contaminated state.
Yuck! I cry, playing along
(he's suspiciously neat at meal-time,
and never messes with his potty.)

But what if something happened
while he was fast asleep;
if I were fried in the fuselage of a small plane
or disappeared into a great foreign war?
Years later he'd tell his therapist,
"Of course, I have no memory
of the man, never really knew him;
I was so young . . ."

Yet here we are: him tossing water into the air
'til he's lifted out kicking,
wanting the bath
to go on forever –
As he hides behind his yellow towel
the two of us carry on like we'll always be a team,
not noticing those thousands
of gleaming soapsuds, snapping.

Miss Karyn McNally's face

Miss Karyn McNally's dark-maned face
appears overnight along Spadina,
painted against a straw-textured background,
on leaflets taped to green steel pillars
by her portraitist, selling lessons in classical art.
It has been raining for three days
and on each leaflet, cold sweat not her own
streaks down her graceful neck
to soak her loose-fitting camel cashmere.
The elements wrinkle her fine features.
They paste MILK posters over her
yet she pushes through,
and each weekend her dogged artist
returns to post a fresh round of Karyns.

To the south, in an odd month for publicity,
William Jefferson Clinton marked the White House
with sperm that sent Republican wolves
into a frenzy.
Yet, something about the face of the fallen Adonis
from a place called Hope
displayed in a million aspects of contrition
kept raising his standing in the polls.
I think of this on my way to work
and of young Monica's ubiquitous face.

How many will take down
Miss McNally's portraits plastered
across the city's lampposts as though she were Wanted
for their own private viewing:

marginal men, starved for a woman's touch,
businessmen too harrowed to recall
the image of a young wife,
all walking past a female gaze
that radiates the vulnerable dignity
of one forced to hold a pose.

How sorely wanted is your beauty
on this loveless damp winter day.

ORDER IN THE CONDO

Order has been restored.
Since the day he inexplicably turned orange,
Pedro, my partner Tom's three foot iguana
with sharp teeth and lashing tail
no longer patrols the guest room we surrendered.
Now, like a piece of kinetic sculpture
he postures and poses in his new floor-to-ceiling pen
that ate up the dining-room 'el'.
Still, when I approach he charges
with bulging eyes and puffed wattles,
macho immigrant to a cold country
having to settle for less than his home in the sun.

Similarly displaced, my own
Santa Maria, the Maltese,
kept swallowing $600 fur balls
and setting off my asthma.
Inhalers neutralized her nights on my pillow.
When she deserted, on doctor's orders I settled for
Iggy, the non-allergenic *bichon frise,*
a lovable matted dust-mop with legs,
but on one walk he broke loose, and I lost him,
another big-city casualty.

These days Tom is never home,
styling hair into the wee hours
or off somewhere with his guy friends
or his personal trainer,
running up frightening VISA bills.

Last week, on a lonely night,
after a day of sending off résumés,
I heard the wire cage rustle and looked up:
Pedro's long curved talons raised him
to human-eye level. He hissed

three words perhaps confessional
but more likely aimed at me.
Just three words, twice
through closed eyes, head nodding mechanically
as if to launch them up my spine:
childless by choice, he hissed – *childless by choice*.

THE WOUND
for Joseph Brodsky

At a graduate student book sale
I found a weighty collection of essays, *Less Than One.*
On the back cover a leonine photo of you,
you still had hair
and looked just this side of annoyed.
They had stuck a price tag across your left upper forehead
that read $16.99,
more than I paid for your remarkable company.
I turned the book over to calculate the mark-up,
(there's always a mark-up from the U.S. to Canada –
let alone darkest Russia,
far in excess of exchange rates.)
I began peeling the tag, not knowing
its gummy backing would refuse to lift
but rather, came off like onionskin,
leaving a white film,
a shrapnel wound to your head,
a clump of old matted bandages
at which I scraped with my nails
for the better part of an hour, trying to free
the Nobel laureate brow,
wondering, do I dare use water?
What if I want to make a gift of this book
when I'm through, as if one ever has enough
of a mind like yours.
I will work away, till I reclaim the image
of a better writer, a propriety
for which you would have had little use,
having borne your wounds
as a matter of fact.

Evening prayers in August

Tonight I am a man
vacationing with family,
the caseload a distant memory.
A folding cot claims the floor space
in this dark cramped motel, forces me
to read in the bathroom,
perched on the toilet lid
in a patch of orange light
while my daughter tries
to push off into sleep.
Soon she and my wife
will be breathing in synchrony,
our son one room down the hall
with his grandpa
already sleeping so deeply
that tomorrow he'll ambush me
with wakefulness.

Chlorine eats at my eyes.
Whatever my antibiotic can't kill,
this motel pool will.
Unable to turn on more light,
or resort to the joys
of wasting kleenex and water,
my thoughts drift
to evils that can follow us anywhere –
when suddenly a finger of white light
slices my visual field!
I jerk up at the pale garotte
across the shower:
a bone-dry swimsuit
is still laking in one corner,
on the verge of a second
animation!

OPEN CASKET

She presides over the red-carpeted parlor,
reinforced by her five devoted sisters
who pass around photos from better days.
The bearded doctor, a guest of her sister Michelle,
grows pale, his own tradition frowning
on preserving the husk, on efforts to transform
our final stony paste into a figure from a wax museum.

"Would you like to come see Nadine?"

He demurs, but steps forward, having never met her alive,
this remarkable lawyer.
Spreading cancer took four years to vanquish
her determined drive to remain,
bones crumbling, iron rods reinforcing hips,
and then neck.

The spectre in lipstick and cropped hair,
flat-chested without prostheses,
seems asleep in her eternal dress-suit
beneath elegant white flowers.
He considers lifting her thin wrist
as if to seek the missing pulse,
her fingers gloved by a second skin.

"Nadine fancied herself an athlete,"
whispers the oldest sister, Marianne.
"She insisted we blend for her those carrot drinks
till the end, and we were happy to.
Once she learned how to walk again,
we couldn't keep her away from her gardening.

She may have needed a walker,
but she could still surf the net and plan the family vacations.
Finally she dropped, after a fall from her bed,
perhaps during a dream."

As they turn, Michelle takes his arm.
"I'm not sure," he says, "about such open display."

"We can see her, touch her. Kiss.
We can feel her gone."
A child hesitates, touches her mother's shoulder
with reverence, then dashes off
to keep up with her cousins.

DUNGENESSQUE

Dungeness, Washington, The Olympic Peninsula

Crack me open like a crab
amused at the strange soft fur along my shell.
Tour my body
find the emotional limits,
dredge my character
for small signs of pretense;
you know they're there.
Haven't others glimpsed claws
beneath my hands?
You listen so closely,
stretching out my present against my past
on your long net,
laying bare . . .

Boil me live
in a scalding caldron
like you would a crab,
turning your head
as the claws fold silently
and you wait for the soft clicking sound.
You can eat me tonight
or tomorrow, or the next night.
because the cooking's done;
all that's left is to analyze
what can and can't be eaten.
Tomorrow you and your analyst
will pick through the bowl of white flesh
from my brittle compartments.
There may be a joke or two,
"Who'd have thought such a slight man
would have so much meat in him?"

SOMEWHERE HALF-FORGOTTEN

Somewhere
half-forgotten
though unforgettable, lost in the debates
on exactly when and where to start him
in junior kindergarten,
somewhere far beyond the lists
of daycares in church and temple basements,
rec centers, private homes,
unlikely corporate
headquarters –

something elemental, like
that look of recognition he beamed
when Grandpa, away these past six months,
appeared
at the arch of the family room,
hair so silvery white and a smile so broad
you knew he wouldn't be footing the bills
or drawing up the game plan
for the next eighteen years.

They had nothing to do but react
to each other, to take
each other in
like the deep orange shine on a bay
meant for visiting.

COMET SOUP

After four throbbing days
of sinuses ballooning my skull,
I grab raincoat and umbrella
and risk pneumonia for Pho Hung.
The owner can spot a desperate diner
and signals his daughter to serve me.

Hunched over my meal in a neighborhood
without dry cleaners on every corner,
I inhale the vapors of seething comets
trailing long slippery tails through a universal broth,
scoop deeper for ghost-balls with a porcelain spoon
concave its full length
and pierce their rice-noodle chambers
for a starburst of peppery pork
that steams open long-sealed passages
suffusing my secular Jewish brain
with Eastern spices and MSG,
un-battening the hatches
of all eight teeming berths, till my eyes pour, unsure
if this be therapy or sin.

RENOVATION
"This kitchen has to go."

After forty years, the cupboard doors,
with hinges known only to the ancients,
threatened to come off in our hands.
Heavy, reluctant pull-out drawers
menaced an unstable back, while
"These days drawers glide in and out
smooth as butter."
A wedged silver tray became immured,
patterns on the vinyl floors were faint memories.

Natural maple cabinets have been chosen,
golden blonde veneer on pressed wood,
"stronger than the real thing."
The trustworthy double sink will soon be scrapped
for a larger major sink with a smaller twin sidekick,
the brown pearl granite and tumbled marble back-splash,
now on order,
will outlive us, and our kids.

More physical men
with better backs at forty, even fifty,
haul drywall, breathe fumes,
and grapple with fridge and stove.
One evening, during a lull in operations,
two cleanly broken potsherds shine through,
threaded with black straps
that might have bound the wrists of a Samson.
Their identical smooth surfaces
turn out not to be clay, after all,
but molded rubber
used by carpenter, painter, or flooring-man,
whatever lord of the quarter-round now loose
inside our palace gates.

At the Temple during Days of Awe,
the senior rabbi jostled pillars of the community
by condemning the diversion of funds
from good-works to kitchen cabinetry.
In today's *Globe*, a man recounts
how he renovated his face:
eyelids trimmed, chin-angle adjusted,
fat harvested from his thighs
to realign his cheeks,
protruding ears pinned.
"He should have tried some nice glasses,
maybe a beard."

After four weeks of chaos,
there will be four more.
Disarmed, we flee with our children up north,
leaving behind oriental carpets tied in bundles.
How many workmen have copies of our key?

"The nicest thing about having a modern kitchen,"
I tell my Princeton-educated wife of twenty years,
"is not only will the food taste better,
but neither of us will ever die."
She feigns a grimace.
Has she overlooked
the small cairn of knee-guards
I mistook for pottery
beside the condemned fridge?
Can she not hear the whir and whine
as loyal appliances protest the surrender
to their betters in stainless steel?

A PORTRAIT OF MY FATHER

Dad, it's me, the *klayner,*
your "little one"
(forget for now the lewd meaning of the word.)
This morning from the last person's flush
a spectral white carnation
unraveled in the bowl,
three-ply, the sort of nicety for which you had little use;
it was never memorialized
in those Twenties, Thirties and Forties songs
you so loved to sing.
It's like Hea-ven when I'm – near you!
It would be Pa-ra-dise – near you!
Once, you sang Louis-Prima-style
I-I-I ain't got No-body!
and a work mate chortled,
Sammy, you got body all right,
beeg body, har har har!

You stoked your insomnia with late-night Coke,
wearing only what, years later, a patient of mine
called "a wife-beater shirt."
Your pregnant belly barely supported
on legs as thin as my own,
in baggy white briefs so tattered
the undershirt's length was a mercy.

You would rather be pictured
dressed in a black CP Rail windbreaker
over a work shirt and well-creased olive pants,
crouching in the union photo
alongside the other baggage checkers.

You weren't yet heavy,
blood pressure was normal,
you hadn't started those pills
that turned your brain to a desert.
You had a pretty 27-year-old wife
(a bit old for those days).

No wonder you were smiling, bright-eyed
beside Buchholtz, Prokopchuk and Rowdan
 – not a Jew in the bunch, but work buddies
who didn't use "Jew" as a verb to your face
unless they'd had one too many.

Neither buddies nor mates, you and I
Never tossed a ball back and forth
 – what older brothers were for –
even in the shallow lake's splashing contests
exchanging no more than a rare wave
during "peace treaties" I declared,
but promptly broke, hysterical with laughter.
You fell backwards, lolling silently nearby,
Monstro, a great pink whale
on his back,
catching your breath.

God rest you, Father,
who checked out at 56,
crooner, punster,
or overmedicated monster,
hear the call of your deep-sea diving son
who navigated your obstacle course to manhood
and would replay the game of hit-and-miss
for a heartfelt hug at the end,
a sincere, if sloppy kiss.

ANT AND APHID
for Robert Frost

Along a cedar crosspiece on my garden gate,
they move slowly past,
a carpenter ant lugs a bright green aphid
waving its legs weakly in the breeze,
and climbs the thick stalk of ivy
towards its nest under the warm wet eaves.

This tiniest of nature's victims farmed for honeydew,
slave labor to an ant, is its life a work history,
even if no clock was punched?
After its sudden, violent sacrifice
will co-religionists obsessively scour the garden square
for signs of massacre remains?
Have not hired ladybugs, headstrong and pretty
as gaily painted tanks carried out ethnic cleansing?

A red winged songbird swoops down, plucks both ant and prey
from the ivy and soars skyward, in miraculous ascent.

This morning, awakening, I knew I no longer had skin,
that anything or anyone who passed my way would move me,
the world's pain as much as its beauty.

But look! The solar clematis sprung up along the fence
are beaming apricot-white faces,
petals boldly unfurled,
determined as any natural thing
whose hours are numbered.

But a clematis is no heal-all,
an ant is not a spider and an aphid not a moth;
in an image all too random, we turn spiders into carpenters,
spin free verse out of rhyme, in literary time;
in a dazzling transformation, a superficial sign.

THREE BUSKERS

In a station of the subway
the smiling old Chinese
alternates between mournful erhu and celestial flute
while the exiled Russian lifts a violin
to tackle Paganini with a long black bow
between trains.

On the other side of the platform,
an overweight reformed alky
honks "Amazing Grace"
repeatedly on a sour horn,
relying on pity to fill his cup.

Near the exit, the pale man in dreadlocks
and a dearth of talent attempts songs
consigned to the dust heap of pop musical history.
He stands harmlessly strumming an acoustic guitar,
subtly eyeing his near-empty hat,
but no one tosses him a wish,
for no one wants to call him
mon semblable or *mon frère.*

High School Concert

After the work day, we scramble
to find the auditorium and catch what remains,
passing rustic murals dedicated
to the fallen young of both great wars.
We've missed the welcoming "Fiesta Nueva",
but take our seats as resonant cannons rattle
in the "Britannia" piece,
then drown in thunderous applause
as the perspiring tuxedoed teddy bear .
turns to take his bow.

There he is, in the front row, our own boy,
strawberry-tipped spikes on a chemical blonde.
It must be hot for him under those high beams,
down here too, as mothers fan themselves
with their programs.

Twin Oprahs, emcees Letisha and Temika
warn us to get out our handkerchiefs for the vocal quartet,
its "For the Beauty of the Earth"
and "Bridge over Troubled Waters"
seamless as poured coffee
could make even a jealous poet cry.

Such transformations:
these offspring with corrected teeth
dipping into classical wells we nearly lost;
the kid with Tourette's syndrome
squeezing his twitchy restlessness
through the bell of a trombone;
a wistful loner who chimes in dreamily on xylophone;
as a strapping brush-cut of a youth
being scouted by the National League

crashes cymbals,
and a lovely graduate performs a soaring solo on flute
too polished to have been born
of band classes alone.

To all the wonderful parents
who drove these kids in the wee morning hours,
Thank you, chime Letisha and Temika.
(Our own boy woke himself at six a.m.,
made breakfast, and scanned the sports page
before he left us still in bed.)

That's him, the one with the gelled hair,
strawberry-tipped spikes on a chemical blonde,
seated in the first row, but wisely
taking his place in the musical background,
on unfaltering clarinet,
foot tapping time, enjoying, I suspect,
the sheer counting exercise of it all.
It's a peppy civility, counterpoint
to the pastoral murals
of the fallen young
of both great wars.

VISITATIONS

Last night I awakened to pounding at my door
and a menace of infectious laughter.
It was The Coach, with eight strapping kids,
and my son the group was after.
All had hazel eyes and sandy hair
and wore uniforms with a Gothic "D"
on the back, a corporate logo.
I tried to feign no surprise.
"It'd be a shame," he said,
"if an athletic kid like yours
missed out on a chance to play.
We practice Friday nights. Games are on Saturdays.
If he trains real hard, one day it just might pay."

When they left, I fell back to dreaming
only to wake to a ballet troupe
come to spirit away my daughter.
There were willowy girls with graceful necks and long limbs
costumed in black Danskins and pink pointe shoes.
"Ze dance," said the Artistic Director, "is a Tree of Life.
It would be a shame that an elegant girl like yours
forfeit the pirouette and *le grand* jété.
If she's devoted, she'll one day command the stage.
We rehearse in the Church daycare up the street
on Friday nights. Performance is on Saturdays."

In a sweat I lurched from light sleep
to still more knocking at the door.
This time it was an earnest young Rabbi
carrying a sacred book.
He too had come for my children.
"It would be a shame," he said, "if bright children like yours
missed out on learning how to pray.
Our services are on Friday nights,
and we begin at ten on the Sabbath Day."

His book unfolded into a Torah scroll
and I asked him to stay,
but he gave me a look of pity,
his eyes grown heavy-lidded
as he became The Old Rabbi in a greatcoat.
Come in, *Rebbe,* for a *glayzeleh tay.*
I sensed he might be the prophet Elijah in disguise
or a Messianic *geist.*

But as I backed into the house
my mind gave in to uneasy sleep,
and I was fading fast in the eyes
of zealots who know
where my family lives,
and who always come to play.

CIRCLE BARBECUE

Three years running, Tom hauls his propane barbecue
to the grassy circle between our three streets.
Everyone's invited to bring kids, desserts and drinks
for a cottage chat in the middle of the city.
Some cancel other events just to be here.

There's talk about the Conservatives
and their vow to eliminate "bureaucrats"
obviously fish-eyed hunchbacks in wigs
who scratch their names on dusty forms
behind thick doors of beveled glass.
Their new party line:
why not have stay-at-home Welfare moms
look after the children of working Welfare moms?
They detest everything about our city,
and ignore its role as engine
of the province's economy.

Chatting over dinosaur paper plates and plastic forks
beneath a clear sky, you avoid asking anyone
'What are you doing these days,"
not wanting to hear about fruitless job searches,
contract work for lousy pay,
or about department store clerks stretched thin
to cover toys and cameras and luggage at the same time
while irate customers clamor for service.
People have a choice: resign or be bought out for their benefits.
Pouring beer into a tall plastic cup, you remember
this nation once was rich in good, secure jobs.
When did it change? When did the CEO and entrepreneur
overtake the minister, the scientist and the physician
as a figure for youthful admiration?

Ah, but this is the circle barbecue,
and even if some yahoo premier from the cold North
has entered the gates of the city, waving
his scythe at weaklings, no-hopers and socialists,
what are we but small-time meadow quarry?

We bite into a long hot dog, twist open a cool one
with the good cheer of free citizens
determined as our young to enjoy a summer's day
whether or not bean-counting horsemen
are on their way.

COTTAGE CLEAN

At the cottage a sweaty T-shirt will do
for another day at the beach,
and in the kitchen, a chipped floor tile,
its gummy-backed grip eased by blasts from a hair dryer,
can be lifted with the cheese slicer.
So what if the bathroom floor around the tub
is a cozy home to earwigs,
if the log chairs with hand-fitted joints
now have more nails in them than wood.
For the young ones a good day means
beach volleyball, lake swims and repainting
the welcome sign.

I meet her on a hiking trail.
"You have grown children?" I ask.
"Well . . . " Her eyes mist over.
She tells of a lively older son
who played the troll under the bridge
to delight the children of guests,
but whom she lost
to low-hanging fog, freshly tinted car windows,
a 'country stop' at an intersection,
and another young man's van,
Rotweiler in the back seat
and no chance to swerve.

"I can talk about it just fine, but here,
every 'keeper' Josh caught stirs memories."
I try to smooth things over with talk of cottage foundations
(hers is concrete block, while ours 'floats'
on two-by-fours over concrete blocks),
then add, "The kids are getting way too much sun."

On this sacred ground, even the rules of science show mercy,
at least off the highway, on resort land
where heavy mists, rising from the lake
obscure the asphalt's cleanly marked lanes,
as determined cars haul canoes on trailers
to the usual escapes.

"HAVE YOU SEEN THIS MAN?
MISSING SINCE JUNE, 2007"

Overnight, outside my office
on the street the signs mushroom,
in large block letters the word "REWARD",
with "offered by family" neatly penned in
above a color photo of a man too vibrant to stay in focus.
In red, his name "Dr. Mitchel Wineberg,
psychiatrist, age 37."

"Last seen Spadina and Bloor
White male, 5'8", 170 lbs., medium build
May go by the name Pancho or Paunchy.
May be wandering disoriented among the homeless.
Feared at risk of suicide."

Mornings later, the dreaded obituary
mentions patients and the homeless
to whom the doctor was especially kind
missing him, along with his dog Farfel
– a curiously personal detail, the name
chosen for the family pet.

Once the circulars spring up,
it is usually too late, the old downward spiral
of discontinuity: psychiatrist, lost soul, missing person.
The shapes in which a man roams the earth
leave a legacy of mushrooming clichés:
How tragic, So young a man,
There but for the Grace of God go I . . .
less the stuff of bulletin than religious brochure
complete with slogan,
"FAR FROM GOD, WHO MOVED?"
and perhaps a computer-generated icon,
the face of a tortured, long-absent prophet,
"HAVE YOU SEEN THIS MAN?"

THE OLD CARDIOLOGY DREAM

Last night I had
the old cardiology dream
of a baby born with six hearts.
So many valves that could falter!
And how rare,
the necessary synchrony.

Baby, I will cherish you,
one-man percussion band that you are,
and devote my life
to seeing yours through.
May none of your frail pink hearts
break mine.

TEMPORARY POWER

He graded my office: "Commanding window,
far from the washrooms . . . nice, very nice"
and, after years of working together,
he offered a transference dream:
"I was flying over jagged cliffs, but with the aid of a minor device."
"To what do you associate?"
"I don't know," he said, looking me over,
"perhaps a microchip."

Sometimes – never at once – we tasted the lakes
of each other's eyes, he assessing, me admiring;
his stunning looks distracting a professional drive
to shore up his flimsy ego. I longed to help him,
though sick at how coldly he spoke of his fiancée.
I thought of the recent 'brown-outs' in Silicon Valley –
and British Columbia helping out with temporary power.

He wore his American ambition like a flag,
at times a Confederate flag that warned of a colossal hurt pride.
Things he carried:
The Wall Street Journal, Fortune, Forbes and *Vanity Fair.*
He parked his SUV "truck" in two of the clinic's parking spaces.
He drank only filtered water, the parched landscape of his casino past
fueled a need to sink pipelines into the terrain of other lives,
impetuously laid and manned by sentries.
Evenings he said the high-tech rosary,
Microsoft, Intel, Cisco and *Oracle,*
and cursed bitterly when the bubble burst
and his margins were called.

Words like *Wuss* and *Wimp* tripped freely off his lips
and stoked the fires of contempt.
His charcoal-gray suits were centered
by silk ties of scarlet and royal blue
that switched on brooding-firmament eyes.

He clung to his parents' survivor guilt
and had "no more use for fiction than for self-help."
I served him in his empire for as long as I was needed,
swept aside by a change of heart,
or of regime?
Years later he described me as "attentive,
very *Canadian*."

BLUE SPERM WHALE

His patient brings in a dream
that infiltrates his office:
I'm about five, I'm on a windy beach
dragging at the sand with my hands,
when suddenly, I bring into view
the rubbery brow of a long-submerged ocean beast.
My fingernails keep clawing, clawing
aching from the pressure,
till after what feels like hours
I unearth its entire body:
it's a blue sperm whale.
But is it alive?

Gingerly, he interprets
her painful struggle to expose
yet somehow contain an old Oedipal menace.
Now, after five years on his taut leather couch,
on a morning in April,
she sits up and confesses, *I love you.*

Other images she shared
speed through his mind:
her mother's horrified scream
when she walked in on them
as her father threw covers over his naked wife,
vague memories of the thrashing that followed,
her back and neck lashed
with the pain of barbed ocean waves
and a terrible excitement.
Now, crowning up through the sand
shamelessly naked and blue,
this spent beast from the sea,
and more, *I love you.*

He recalls that her dreams are often
laced with fish-hooks. Here too,
Each time I try to free their grips
they snare and bite at my fingers.

Mentors from his training
circle like pilot fish
offering a school of evasive replies
from a feeble "I have feelings for you,"
to a simple, suspect "Thank you,"
as if he were gaining, no, maintaining
an upper hand, as in the lament,
The patient has a vantage point,
the therapist an advantage point.

I love you too, trips off his lips
because of a moment's truth,
because the risk of losing his license
seems banal against her gallery of ocean images.
And though he knows she has been raped
and repeatedly mistreated,
(The rapist, she nicknamed a doctor from her past),
he rises from his chair as she rises from his couch
for a long silent hug.

Later he tells a frowning colleague
who specializes in physician abuse,
"Hugging a female patient is never sexual
for me; it only happens from the waist up."

But even as he defends his stance
he senses the stirring head of a blue sperm whale
trying to free itself from the sand.
A nearby buoy shines bright as a cenotaph.
Stretched across the excavated pit
where once a whale tried to surface,
he grieves what little remains, lines of tiny barbs
glistening and twitching in the ocean breeze,
painted with freshly drawn blood.

ELEPHANT STREET
for those who chart the red shift of galaxies

When Israel went forth from Egypt, Andrew and I
wound our way through another spring.
The Jordan turned back a rush of hot-dog smells,
a pollen of street dust and car-stereos blasted through open
windows.
The mountains skipped like rams past panhandlers and boutiques,
and Andrew grinned down at me like a great carnivorous fish.
"Judaism is an aesthetic choice," he said.
The sea saw it and fled.

An expanding universe is speeding up. My step slows.
I had shaken my head: "How can anyone be an atheist?"
"But *you're* an atheist," he cries over the busy intersection.
"There are *hundreds* of Gods you don't believe in
– like the elephant-headed Ganesh, and only *one* in which you do."
We're in for a lovers' quarrel.

I scoured the universe with questions,
scrubbing until it was nearly clean,
but by the *Gates of Prayer* we stopped again to dodge the cars.
Half-heartedly, I switched back to science,
the "eternal molecules" argument, which he side-swiped.
"If a car were to hit you between here and Spadina Avenue,
would your family be consoled
to know your molecules were still around?
You wouldn't be forgotten, but you'd be gone."
The heavens belong to the Lord, but the earth is given to mortals:
That made me look around and count
the number of streets on which a Jew could walk.

A universe was speeding up when it should slow down.
We parted the seas, as usual, on good terms.
The rock of his heart by then must have been turning to water;
we are just flints from which sparks are struck.
It is not the dead who praise the Lord,
it is not those who go down to silence.

125

It's like that, talking about God over lunch-hour
as the seasons change on the unforgiving concrete.
"To Fate," Andrew calls back a final time,
raising an imaginary wine glass as he steps into traffic,
"no matter how we render it."

THE NIGHT AFTER

The night after I learned
they uncovered a plan to dynamite the day care centre
I reached back in time
for my frail infant son
swaddled in a blanket after ritual circumcision,
and when I found him, I lowered him
into the snow-covered earth of Canada,
then withdrew him, to consecrate
– if the world would allow it –
the life he would lead as a Jewish man
with newborns of his own.

But now the matter rests in Security's poorly paid hands,
and in the Middle East the judgement hour advances
so swiftly that even talk
of "a two-state solution,"
of "building first the wall, then making the peace,"
of "post-Zionism," and forcing both sides to relocate,
– all the talk in this world cannot dampen my fear
of a world bereft of holiness.

Like benediction, relief comes
only from immersion in sleep
and in earth yet unclaimed
by a long-forgotten dream of peace,
a peace that stretches not just from Cairo to Amman
but Baghdad to Riyadh, Beirut to Damascus
– to Jerusalem! –
all the sacred incendiary points between
Salaam and *Shalom.*

ACKNOWLEDGEMENTS

Selections from *The Big Life Painting* ©1987 Ron Charach, Quarry Press (Kingston). Selections from *Someone Else's Memoirs* © 1994 Ron Charach, Quarry Press (Kingston). Selections from *Past Wildflowers* © 1997 Ron Charach, Quarry Press (Kingston). Selections from *Petrushkin* © 1999, 2000 Ekstasis Editions, Victoria. Selections from *Dungenessque* © 2001 Ron Charach, Signature Editions, Winnipeg. Selections from *Elephant Street* © 2003 Ron Charach Signature Editions, Winnipeg.

In the poem "Elephant Street" italicized lines are quoted, with permission, from *Gates of Prayer: The New Union Prayer Book*, copyright 1975 by the Central Conference of American Rabbis.

The author is grateful for editorial input received in the dawn of his career from Andy Patton, during the day from Andy Patton, Janice Gurney, Alice Charach, Colin Morton, Bob Hilderley, and a number of journal editors. In mid-career he received valuable editing from Susan Ioannou, George Amabile, and support for reworking these poems from Maria Jacobs and Noelle Allen of Wolsak and Wynn.